What's So Different About Islam?

My Experience of the Christian World and the Islamic World

By

Linnette James-Sow

Published by New Generation Publishing in 2013

Copyright © Linnette James-Sow 2013

First Edition

The author asserts the moral right under the Copyright, Designs and Patents Act 1988 to be identified as the author of this work.

All Rights reserved. No part of this publication may be reproduced, stored in a retrieval system or transmitted, in any form or by any means without the prior consent of the author, nor be otherwise circulated in any form of binding or cover other than that which it is published and without a similar condition being imposed on the subsequent purchaser.

www.newgeneration-publishing.com

 **New Generation Publishing**

This book is dedicated to my mother, without whom it would have been impossible to put pen to paper to develop this book. Mom, you have been my inspiration!

As I grow older and take on more of life's responsibilities, I often question myself: how I can do things perfectly?

The truth is, I strive to be like my mother when I strive for perfection—because in my eyes, Mother, to be perfect is to be like you.

I realize now that I can never be like my mother, nor can I do everything perfectly.

But, Mother, if I could be three-quarters of the woman you are, half the mother that you are, one quarter of the human being you are, and one eighth of the humanitarian that you are—then, Mother, I know that my purpose here on earth is done.

To my darling daughter, Latifah: your birth has motivated me to new heights. Because of you, I believe I can reach the unreachable. I absolutely love you; you are my world!

To the Eloquent Books publishers and staff: thank you for giving me a chance. I hope to do more work with you in the future.

Table of Contents

Dedication 3
Introduction 7

Chapter 1 9

What is Religion?
What is Christianity?
What is Islam?

Chapter 2 11

My History
My Experience at My First School in England
Our Move to Leicester

Chapter 3 17

The Malicious Gossip
My Loss of Faith in the Church

Chapter 4 23

Contrasts and Comparisons between Islam
    and Christianity Creation
Differences between the Qur'an and the Bible
My Conversion to Islam

Chapter 5 36

My Wedding Day
My Trip to Guinea
My Experience of Muslim Family in England

Chapter 6 42

My Fear for My Daughter
My Marriage
The Internal Conflict
My Hope and for the Future

References 47

Introduction

What's So Different About Islam?

This book highlights my experience growing up as a Christian and converting to Islam. By no means does this book aim to demean or criticize any religion or anyone's beliefs. It represents my personal experience from both worlds, as I have lived it.

I hope this book will be educational to those who are not familiar with religions other than their own. I acknowledge that my individual experience may differ from others' experiences. The manner in which I've depicted my story does not mean to represent the manner in which each individual from both the Christian and the Muslim faith react to religions other than their own.

I hope that my experiences will help others understand the world in which we live and the people around us who pray differently, walk differently, look differently, and have different beliefs, aspirations and dreams.

Chapter 1

What is Religion?

Religion is about having faith and a relationship with God. It's not just a theory, but also a practiced belief. According to allaboutreligion.org, religion is "a belief concerning the supernatural, sacred, or divine, and the practices and institutions associated with such belief." (http://www.allaboutreligion.org/definition-of-religion-fac.htm.)

What is Christianity?

According to Collins Dictionary (1994), 'Christianity is a religion based on the life and teachings of Christ.' Jesus is known as Christ and as the Son of God within the Christian faith. 'Christ' literally means 'the anointed one,' and Christians regard Christ as the Messiah. According to biblical passages, God sent Christ to earth to die for our sins so that we could be forgiven. One of the strongest themes in 'Jesus' teaching whilst he was on earth was about forgiveness (2 Chronicles 7:14). Christianity teaches that there is only one God, and that we should not worship any gods but Him (Exodus 20:3). Christianity also teaches that, 'Jesus Christ is the second person of the trinity, that Jesus died on the cross and rose from the dead physically, [and] that all people are under the righteous judgment of God because all people have sinned against God' cited on

(http://www.carm.org/christianity/answers-seeking/what-christianity).

In most Christian denominations, for one to become a Christian, he must be born again; this means that he must repent of his sins. Then, he must be baptized and change his lifestyle: 'I tell you the truth no one can enter the Kingdom of God unless he is born of water and the spirit.' (John 3:3)

What is Islam?

According to Collins Dictionary (1994), Islam is the 'Muslim religion teaching that there is one God and that Mohammed is his prophet.' Mamood (2008) stated that there are three concepts about Islam: the belief that there is only one God, the belief that He has power that is above and beyond all other forces and sources on earth, and that it's within our own will to be believers or non-believers of His teachings, which He has sent to us through his prophets. One cannot be a true Muslim without accepting and being obedient to the teachings of God of which was revealed to Prophet Muhammad (Ibrahim, 1997). According to the teaching of Islam, when one converts to Islam, God will forgive them of all their sins (Ibrahim, 1997).

Chapter 2

My History

I was born and partly raised in Kingston, Jamaica. My mother was and still is a devoted Christian. I was raised to attend Sunday school and Sunday afternoon worship, which followed shortly afterwards. I always believed in God the Father, and Jesus His son. No one ever challenged me about this, nor did I have any reason to believe that it wasn't true. Growing up in Jamaica, I wasn't aware of any religion other than Christianity. I was raised within the Pentecostal faith and was aware of other denominations within Christianity such as Catholicism and the Baptist faith, which I understood shared a similar belief system to my own.

I was taught that reading my Bible and praying daily would keep me close to God, and that with this closeness, came blessings, anointing, deliverance and protection from all that's ungodly. My mother is a prayer warrior, and I grew up watching her interact with God through prayer. She would say a prayer for everything, from thanking God for our daily bread to asking for His divine blessing in every examination I undertook in school.

I was very successful throughout my school years, firmly believing my success was partly due to my hard work and my mother's prayers. I still believe that. At thirteen years old, I came out first in a class of thirty-five students at my end-of-year report. I continued to perform well in school until I was fifteen.

That was when my prayer warrior migrated to England after getting married. I wasn't able to follow her immediately and had to wait another year, as my mother had to receive her indefinite stay in England before she could apply for me. I resided with one of my aunt (my dad's sister) during this period. My world fell apart. How would I cope without my mom who had anointed me with olive oil and prayed for me daily? I believed in her, and I believed in prayer. I fell from the 'A' class in Jamaica to 'C' class. My foundation had been removed from beneath me; my rock had gone.

A year later, I followed my mother to England. I was so elated, partly because I was going to a country where I thought the sky would be the limit, as I was entering into a country that, by far, had more wealth than that of the country of my origin, but mostly because I would be reunited with my darling mother. I never thought for one minute that catastrophe would befall us.

Upon my arrival in England, I became aware of the diverse cultures and religion there, most of which were new to me. Although Jamaica is varied in its ethnic origin, religious beliefs and practices were not so varied.

My Experience at my First School in England

The religion that struck me the most was the Islamic faith, partly because the women of the Islamic faith dressed in such a unique way. Mostly, I noticed the derogatory comments both the media and my peers made about Islam. A Muslim classmate wanted to be my friend. I liked her, but the other kids in my class informed me that her dad had three wives, and that being her friend wasn't in my best interest; the rest of the school, especially the girls of my own ethnicity, would make my life unbearable.

I thought this was hideous; how could a country known for its freedom of speech and democracy determine who could and couldn't be your friends? I thought, *I am of a strong character; I can give as well as I get.* But then the bullying started. School became a living hell. Inside the classroom, the kids refused to speak to me. Outside the classroom, they picked on me and called me names. Once when it became unbearable, my mother came to collect me from school; the bullies waited outside the school gate to taunt me.

As soon as I saw my mother, I broke down in tears. One of my tormentors saw my tears and seemed shocked by how much hurt the bullies had caused me. It appeared that they didn't want to inflict pain on the level that they had done. However, they had a message to get across.

I returned to school the following day to meet a group of girls standing in the hallway. These were my tormentors. My heart raced and my stomach churned. I wanted to turn around and run away because I thought they were going to physically attack me. Thoughts started to race inside my head. I knew I couldn't take on six bullies. So I went into the toilet. My tormentors went with me and waited outside the door while I locked myself into one of the toilet cubicles. *This is it,* I thought. *I will never be able to see my mother again.* I locked myself in the toilet and refused to come out. It was time for the morning assembly, and they got tired of waiting.

I decided that I wouldn't go to school that day, and I went home in tears. At home, my mother met me at the door with horror on her face, partly because I was supposed to be in school and partly because I was distressed. I explained what had happened. My mother had never seen me this scared before, not even in the rough parts of Jamaica, where I would sometimes go to catch a bus. Mom immediately rang the school and made an appointment to see the school head. I stayed home for the day, but I had to return the following day to see the principal with my mom.

At the school, we knocked on the door. A man I had seen once or twice before welcomed us. I was apprehensive about going into his office because I wasn't sure what we would achieve. *This might make the situation worse,* I thought. *On the other hand, it might scare the bullies into finally leaving me alone.* Mom and I sat down, and Mom began to tell the principal what had happened. The principal then asked me to give my perspective. As I named my tormentors one by one, my confidence grew.

The principal summoned the ringleader to his office. When she saw my mother and I, her face went white as a sheet. The principal asked me to repeat my story. Seeing the bully's anxiety gave me some reassurance, as I told the story. The bully did not deny anything I said, but she was rather apologetic. 'It wasn't my idea,' she explained. 'I really like Linnette,'she further emphasized.

I left the principal's office feeling relieved. When I returned to class, all heads turned to look at me in a questioning manner. However, no one spoke to me. Later that day, one of the girls who often bullied me approached me,. 'Hi Linnette,' she said in a calming voice. 'I just wanted to be your friend.'

I was baffled. How could someone want to be your friend and treat you in such an inhumane manner? 'Why have you been so unkind to me?' I asked.

'I was just annoyed that you were hanging with Ruksana,' she replied. 'I thought that if we were mean to you, then you'd stop being friends with her. We didn't mean for you to be so hurt.'

'What's so wrong about being friends with Ruksana?' I asked.

'She's Muslim. To be friends with her is like colluding with the enemies.'

'Why?' I asked.

'They're evil, and they don't like non-Muslims. They're pompous.'

I didn't make any further challenges. Although I liked Ruksana, I began avoiding her. She would wait for me outside the classroom at lunchtime, and we would walk to the canteen. After this conversation with my newfound friend, Ruksana was always at least three feet behind me, trying to keep up. Not only did I want to fit in, but I also started believing what my classmates said about Muslims.

The relationship between Ruksana and I deteriorated as she realized I was avoiding her. I missed Ruksana, but I liked feeling that I could walk around the school grounds without being taunted. I also liked going home without my mother having to meet me outside the school gates. After all, I was a teenager and was old enough to make my way home. Life at school became more bearable, as I had more friends. However, I remained apprehensive about becoming too friendly with some of the girls who had taunted me.

Our Move to Leicester

When her marriage broke down, Mom decided we would move to a different county. I was excited about this new start. I thought I'd be able to be friends with whom I chose.

Life in Leicester seemed perfect at first. I had a new home, a new school, and a new church. At college, I met a friend from Jamaica—finally, someone who understood my dialect and culture! As we made other friends, I noticed that other students thought it was 'cool' to hang out with us because of our nationality. They would refer to us as 'yardies' (this is a terminology used by some non-Jamaicans when referring to Jamaicans). My friend relished this attention, but being called 'yardie' felt derogatory to me. The yardies were a notorious gang in London. I wasn't part of a gang and had no intention of being apart of one. But other than that, life at college was okay. I hardly met anyone of the Muslim faith.

I finished college successfully and embarked on studying at a higher level. It was during this period that I received a song-writing contract and I immediately withdrew from my study, as I thought that I was going to become rich. I tried to pursue a career in this genre of writing, confident that I was going to be successful.

However, as time went by, I realized that my dream was fast diminishing. Not only was I spending money on production and advertisement, but I was also sending a lot of my creative work to agents without achieving any recognition or royalty.

I decided to go back to college, this time to study nursing. During my break from school, I had been working as a healthcare assistant and found the job to be rewarding.

Chapter 3

The Malicious Gossip

During this period, the social circle around my mother and me started to disintegrate. A cousin of my mother who lived in the same county as ourselves had started spreading malicious rumors about us. This cousin and my mother belonged to the same church, so I thought the church would rectify the injustice. I never thought the church would become my mom's cousin's biggest supporter. Mom and I were newcomers to this particular church, whilst our cousin has been a member of this church for many years. Her husband was also a pastor of one of the adjoining church, which made us outsiders and easy targets to prey on. Mom's presence would be ignored at church. If she should attempt to participate in any programmes at church, they would mock her Jamaican dialect (considering that the members of this church are predominantly Jamaicans.) They would also whisper and snigger amongst themselves as she would pass by. Eventually, Mom was stopped from performing or playing any part in Sunday services. That's when my faith in the 'church' began to wane. My mother and I had no refuge; we couldn't walk the streets in peace without people pointing at us, and we couldn't feel the presence of God at church anymore. Instead, church had become a circus and a battlefield.

We were ostracized, tried and convicted even though my mom's cousin had no real substance to her stories. In the Caribbean, it would have been the pastor's job to call the individuals in question and investigate the reason behind the conflict. But in my mom's case, the malicious gossip became a sermon

Sunday after Sunday.

I decided to stop attending church. I couldn't stand to see the way people who claimed to be followers of God treated my mom. I had learned that God was love and peace, and that everyone who followed Him should try to be like Him. Where was the love and peace in this church? According to my upbringing, the church was meant to set an example for all to follow. How could this church encourage people to do good while it incited hatred? *What hypocrites,* I thought.

Amongst the hurt and malicious rumors, I started college for the third time. There, I met Ibrahim. I had no idea where he was from, nor did I ask questions about his religion. Amongst all the pain that was being inflicted on my mother and me, this seemed trivial. Ibrahim and I developed a friendship.

One day, a colleague asked me, 'Do you know Ibrahim is a Muslim?' I was shocked on receiving this information. I wanted to confront Ibrahim to find out the truth but I was too scared of hearing the unexpected, as I wasn't sure how this would affect our relationship due to the manner in which I was treated when Ruksana was my friend. Weeks went by before I could finally find the courage to confront Ibrahim and ask him if he was Muslim.

I asked Ibrahim if this was true. 'Yes,' he said.

'Why did you keep it a secret?' I asked.

'Are you of any faith?' he asked.

'Yes, I am Christian,' I responded.

'Why did you keep it a secret?'

'You didn't ask,' I replied.

'Well, you didn't ask me my religion, either,' said Ibrahim, 'so why would I spontaneously inform you?'

I suddenly realized that I had expected my friend of the Islamic faith to wear his religion on his forehead. I wasn't openly or consciously judgmental, but unconsciously, I was. How could I allow my distorted perception to determine another human being's character? Should someone not be judged by his behavior and character, rather than the way others perceive him? This was what the 'church' had been doing to my mom and me. How could I pass on this same treatment to someone else?

I made a conscious decision not to let Ibrahim's religion interfere with our friendship. I tried to convince myself it didn't matter. As our friendship grew, I realized that Ibrahim was one of the most genuine and loyal friends I'd ever had. He supported my song-writing career, even though secular songwriting wasn't acceptable in his religion, as it was seen as promoting the work of the devil. He read the songs I wrote and encouraged me to try and get them published. He even sat with me in the computer suite to help me type my essays, as my typing skills weren't very good. I wondered what the fuss was all about. Did these people who were so anti-Muslim ever take the opportunity to look beyond someone's religion?

My Loss of Faith in the Church

In the meantime, the condemnation that surrounded Mom and me continued to grow. Mom had been raised by her grandfather, who was a dedicated Baptist minister. He was prophetic and saw events before they occurred. He had encouraged Mom not only to attend church on Sundays, but also to live a lifestyle that was considered acceptable in God's eyes. But one day, I asked Mom if she ever thought that she had been brainwashed into believing there was a God, in turn brainwashing me.

Mom was astounded by my comment. For her, the one thing that had remained rock solid was her faith.

She believed the tribulation we were going through was a testament to our faith, and that, like Job, we would emerge victorious at the end.

'If there's a God, Mom, why does He sit back and allow us to suffer like this?' I asked.

Mom began to tell me the biblical stories of Daniel and how he was thrown into the lions' den without the lions harming him (Daniel 6: 16–23). She mentioned Shadrach, Meshach and Abednego, who were all thrown in the fiery furnace without being scathed (Daniel 3; 19–26). Finally, she got to Job, who had suffered for many years. He had lost all his livestock and his children (Job, 2001), and his skin broke out in sores. Mom said, 'Job never lost faith, even after his wife told him, 'let's curse God and die' (Job 2:9). In the end, God rewarded Job for his faith by giving back every thing he had lost in abundance twice over (Job 42:10–16).

I broke down in tears, feeling like Job's wife. I resented the church for the way they had destroyed my faith. They had broken my spirit. Like Mom, I'd had such a firm belief in God; I believed that it was impossible to achieve anything in life without His intervention. And now, I was questioning His existence. I felt that I had let my mother down, that I had betrayed her.

My struggle affected my college work, and I became worried I wouldn't complete the course successfully. But whilst at college, I had a source I could rely on: Ibrahim. We did our research together, comparing our findings and sharing information. After completing each assignment, Ibrahim and I went through one another's work and gave feedback. This kept me motivated. I finished college successfully and enrolled to undertake a BSc degree in mental health nursing. Ibrahim enrolled in the same university six months later.

We continued to support and encourage each other. During my three years at university, I remained in emotional turmoil. But I was determined that I wouldn't let the church rob me of my education. 'I am doing this for Mom,' I kept telling myself.

Toward the end of our university study, Ibrahim and I started to discuss religion. He spoke about Islam with conviction. He believed in what he was saying, and he was proud of his religion. However, I couldn't help but notice the pain in his eyes when the topic about the media's portrayal of Islam came up, as well as the perceptions non-Muslims held of Muslims. 'It saddens me that through ignorance, we are all tainted with the same brush,' he said. 'Islam isn't about hate and war; it emphasizes love and peace.'

I didn't feel the same pride in my religion. I felt proud about how my mother had raised me. She had instilled in me the value of respecting others and myself.

Nonetheless, I had a solid knowledge about the Bible and was able to speak about it. I told Ibrahim how my mother had ensured that I attended Sunday school, Sunday services, and Bible school whilst I was growing up in Jamaica. Ibrahim was impressed that a non-Muslim girl had, had an upbringing that one could be described as being 'pure.' We started to make a connection on a different level. Although we were raised in different parts of the world, I felt as though the same individual had raised us both. Our morals, work ethics, dreams and future plans were so similar to one another's.

Our conversations helped me realize I wasn't angry at Christianity itself. I didn't harbor any grudge, bitterness or hatred towards the doctrine of the Bible. I still had my faith, although it occasionally got weak. It was the people calling on the name of God and publicly declaring the love of God to win souls that angered me. How could they kill one person's spirit whilst pretending to win others? How could they spread so much hatred and malice and then speak about love? It all seemed so contrived.

However, religion became part of our conversation whenever we would meet. I became very interested in the teachings of Islam; they reminded me of Bible scriptures. Ibrahim was also interested in my upbringing. He hadn't met many Afro-Caribbeans from a Christian background, and I guess he was surprised that we weren't that different after all.

Chapter 4

Contrasts and Comparisons between Islam and Christianity

Creation

One thing was missing in my life. I had stopped praying, as I didn't see the purpose. My mom still cried out to God in prayer two or three times per day. She fasted on a weekly basis, whilst the lies and scandal created by fellow churchgoers continued. I felt as though there was a void within me. Ibrahim often went to the Mosque to pray. I envied him. We continued to talk about religion, comparing and contrasting the Islamic and Christian faiths.

Although there were differences, I was surprised to learn there were so many similarities. The two religions share some terminology and some theology. I was surprised that the omnipotent and omnipresent creator of heaven and earth (Genesis 1:1) was the same God the Islamic faith referred to as *Allah*: 'God is the one who raised the Heavens up without any visible support. Then He mounted the Throne and regulated the Sun and the Moon; each runs along on a specific course. He directs the matter; He manifests signs so that you may be convinced about meeting you Lord' (Thunder : 2–3, p320).

I began to question the Christians around me, some of whom attended the same university as myself and some of whom were the very individuals that were spreading vicious rumours about my mother. I tried to highlight the fact that the Qur'an and the Bible had similar doctrines, but I would be rebuked. 'How can you compare the Bible to the Qur'an?' Christians often asked me. One woman said that I had blasphemed against God. I felt as though I had been hit by lightening. According to the Bible, blasphemy is one sin that can never be forgiven (Matthew 12:31). I feared my life, my soul, and my entire being was doomed to hell.

But as Ibrahim and I continued to speak about Christianity and Islam, I became more convinced I wasn't doomed. I hadn't blasphemed, for to blaspheme is to speak disrespectfully of God, and that was never my intention. As I sought clarification about why Christians saw Muslims as their enemies, I realized that some of it was simply due to lack of knowledge about the Qur'an.

Ibrahim and I studied the creation of Adam and Eve. The Bible documents how God went about creating man: 'The Lord God formed the man from the dust of the ground and breathed into his nostrils the breath of life, and the man became a living being' (Genesis 2:7). The Islamic faith held the same belief: 'He began by creating man from clay; then He made his progeny from an extract of discarded waste; next, He completed him and breathed some of His own spirit into him' (Worship 32:4–9, p555). Both religions paralleled one another's creation stories. Unlike me, Ibrahim wasn't shocked by the similarities between our faiths; he was well familiar with these teachings.

So why do non-Muslims believe they are so indifferent from those of the Islamic faith? Could it be because so few people take the time to read the verses of the Qur'an that emphasize these similarities? Or are we just blinded by the broadcasted terror of a handful of extremists? In actuality, Islam is a religion that promotes peace and mercy. 'The first cases to be adjudicated between people on the Day of Judgment will be those of bloodshed' (Ibrahim,1997, p 60).

The Bible spoke about the creation of earth: 'In the beginning God created the heavens and the earth. Now the earth was formless and empty, darkness was over the surface of the deep, and the Spirit of God was hovering over the waters' (Genesis 1:1–2 NIV) Genesis further emphasizes the darkness that covered earth and how God changed this by saying, 'Let there be light'— and 'there was light' (Genesis 1:3). Furthermore, Genesis tells us that 'The light God called day, and the darkness, He called night' (Genesis 3:5).This story is reflected in the Qur'an. 'He is the one who spread out the earth and placed mountains and rivers on it, and has placed two pairs for every kind of fruit on it. He merges daylight into night. In that are signs of those who reflect' (Thunder 13:2–3, p320).

Growing up, I would read the biblical story about Satan and his descent from heaven. Islam upholds this same belief. Satan was cast aside by God after refusing to follow God's command: 'Get out from this (Paradise), disgraced and expelled. Whoever of them (mankind) will follow you, then surely I will fill Hell with you all' (The Heights 7:18, p 201). Speaking with Ibrahim, I felt as though I was in Sunday school allover again. Although I was learning about the Qur'an instead of the Bible, the teachings felt no different. We were worshippers of the same God.

The beliefs of some Christians

Many Christians believe Muslims worship Mohammad the prophet instead of God. This perception comes from lack of knowledge of the Islamic faith. If one reads the Islamic sacred books, he/she will see the emphasis on Mohammed as a prophet, carrying out the work of God with His permission, again and again.

The beliefs of some Muslims.

On the other hand, Muslims do not believe in the Bible, even though there are so many similarities between the two holy books. Muslims believe that the scriptures of the Bible are not original and have been altered in one way or another (Ibrahim, 1997, p59). A committee of thirty-two scholars revised the Holy Bible, giving this quote: 'Notes are added which indicate significant variations, additions, or omissions in the ancient authorities (Mt 9:34; Mk 3:16;7:4; Lk 24:32, 51, etc. Ibrahim, p. 59).

The forgiveness of sins

The Bible claims that after one has repented of his sins and become a born-again Christian, God will forgive him all his sins (John 3:3). This added credibility to my experience on the day I converted, for according to the Qur'an, 'But as for him who repented (from polytheism and sins), believed (in the Oneness of Allah, and His Messenger Muhammad, and did righteous deeds (in the life of this world), then he will be among those who are successful" (Tales 20:67, p525).

The Christian faith believes that God will return to earth with fire on judgment day and that those who believe in Him and call on His name shall be spared this judgment (Malachi 4). (Matthew 8:11) also reflects this sentiment: 'I say to you that many will come from the east and the west, and will take their places at the east with Abraham, Isaac and Jacob in the Kingdom of Heaven. But the subjects of the Kingdom will be thrown outside, into the darkness, where there will be weeping and gnashing of teeth.' Similarly, the Qur'an states that, 'If you could but see when they are set before the fire [hell] and say, 'Would that we might return (to the world)! Then we would not reject the verses of our Lord, but we would be of the believers!' (Qur'an, 6:27, p173).

The Christian faith believes in one God (Corinthians 8:6), and Islam emphasizes this same belief: 'And he is Allah, none has the right to be worshipped but He) all praises and thanks be to Him (both) in the first and in the last' (Tales 28:70, p525).

My beliefs

With all these similarities, I find it difficult to believe the two faiths aren't worshipping the same God. Some might call me naive, and some might even say my husband has brainwashed me. But I have done my research; I have interacted with individuals of the Islamic faith.

I was born and raised a Christian, and I am convinced that the God the Christian world refers to as God the Lord, the Creator of heaven and earth, is the same God the Islamic world refers to as Allah. There are differences between the faiths that I have found difficult to accept; however, the basic teachings are the same. For that reason, I am happy to say that I have found an anchor. I can pray and have faith again, knowing there is a divine presence looking after my well-being.

Differences between the Qur'an and the Bible

The Bible speaks about Jesus as the Son of God (John 5:22). It's unheard of within the Christian faith to believe in God but not His Son, and vice-versa. Matthew 11:27 explains that, 'All things have been committed to me by my Father. No one knows the Father except the Son and those to whom the Son chooses to reveal Him.' The Islamic faith doesn't share the belief in the oneness of God and Jesus: 'Allah the Self-Sufficient Master, Whom all creatures need, (He neither eats nor drinks). He begets not, nor was He begotten. And there is none co-equal or comparable unto Him' (Sincerity 112:2–4, p854–855).

I have struggled to accept this belief, as I was raised to believe in God the Father, Jesus, His Son and God the Holy Spirit, the three in one (1 John 5:1–12). I still hold this belief, as not having it would bring utter devastation to me. Not being able to say 'in Jesus' name' when I pray is comparable to not being able to inhale clean air. For me, the statement 'in Jesus' name' has power. It can and has cast out demons and cured physical ailments.

The Qur'an goes on to say, 'Surely, they have disbelieved who say: 'Allah is the Messiah, son of Maryam' (Qur'an, 5:72, p 158). According to the Qur'an, those who believe that God is associated with any other will not see the promise land: 'Children of Israel, worship God, my Lord and your Lord. Whoever associates partners in worship with God, then God has forbidden Paradise for him, and his home is the Fire (hell). For wrong doers, there will be no helpers' (Qur'an, 5:72 p 158).

The Christian faith believes that Jesus was born of the Virgin Mary, who carried him until birth, but the Qur'an doesn't share the notion. The Qur'an documents Jesus being created in the same format as Adam: 'Verily, the likeness of 'Isa (Jesus) before Allah is the likeness of Adam. He created him from dust, then (He) said to him: "Be!"—and he was.' (Qur'an, 3:59, p77).

The Islamic faith also does not share the belief that Jesus was crucified. They believe that there was a plot to kill Jesus, but that God saved him from his enemies: 'And because of their saying (in boast), 'We killed

Messiah 'Isa (Jesus), son of Maryam, the Messenger of Allah, but they killed him not, nor crucified him, but it appeared the resemblance of 'Isa (Jesus) was put over another man (and they killed that man), and those who differ therein are full of doubts. They have no conjecture. For surely; they killed him not' (Qur'an, 4:157, p136).

Some of the practices amongst the Islamic and the Christian faith

Another difference between Islam and Christianity are the postures used during prayer. I'm used to praying aloud whilst kneeling or standing. When praying to God in Islam, one mutters under his breath in Arabic—a language I do not understand. Therefore, it makes it difficult for me to know what a prayer is about.

Christians often pray about a specific subject. . When Christians put in a prayer request about their needs and those needs are met, then they can say, 'God has performed a miracle; He's answered my prayer.' Sometimes, God manifests Himself through His Spirit (1 John 5:7), and during intercession with Him, you can feel His presence in His Spirit. Almost any Christian who has lived a life acceptable to God can speak about this experience.

I was nine years old when I had my first encounter with God's presence. It's a normal practice for church leaders to perform an 'altar call' at the end of Sunday worship. This is a process in which both members and non-members of the church who are having difficulty in their lives make their way to the altar for prayer. They would walk right to the front of the church, whereby a designated person or persons would lay their hands on them, anoint them with olive oil and intercede on their behalf to God.

I rarely walked to the altar, and when I did, it was normally under duress from my mother. As a shy child, I hated being the focus of attention. However, one day, I spontaneously decided to go to the altar without my mother's intervention. I had an eye problem that caused me to blink excessively, and I was unable to see objects from afar. The eye specialist at the time diagnosed me with shortsightedness, and I had to wear glasses. Whilst these helped me to see farther distances, they did not help with my blinking. So I went forward for healing on my eyes. I vividly remember my Sunday school teacher coming over and resting her hand on my shoulder. She began to pray: 'Lord, you know why Linnette is at the altar.' I responded quietly, 'Lord, I am here for my eyes to be healed.' I immediately felt a warm sensation running through my body, starting from the top of my head and continuing to the end of my toes.

I told my mother what I had felt and asked for her opinion. I was so accustomed to over-blinking that I didn't realize I wasn't doing it much whilst I spoke to my mother. My blinking had returned to normal. 'You're healed!' my mother screamed. 'You're not blinking as fast anymore.' I immediately took off my glasses to test how far I could see, finding that I didn't need them anymore. My mom took me back to see the eye specialist. He didn't have an explanation for what had occurred, and Mom and I did not disclose God's miracle to him. From that day onwards, I have never worn prescribed glasses again.

Although it's difficult to know what one is praying about in Islam, I admire and respect the postures that individuals take when conducting their prayer, in which they ensure that their foreheads touch the floor. I initially queried this style of praying. After discussions with my husband, I couldn't agree more with the format Muslims use during prayer. My husband and I agree that because God is unique and incomparable, then it's only right that He be worshipped in a manner that demonstrates total respect for Him.

Islamic events attended

Apart from the day of my conversion and my daughter's naming, I have never again visited a mosque. However, my husband attends what is called the 'Qur'an day' every month, facilitated by the people of his culture and religion. It's a form of worship whereby men, women and children of the Islamic faith congregate to worship and socialize. The men sit at one end of the room whilst the women sit on the other side with their children. The men read the Qur'an and pray in Arabic, whilst the women speak amongst themselves until mealtime. Then the women serve the men and themselves.

This form of worship has no meaning to me, partly because I can't understand what's being said, but mostly because there is no music. It seems like more of a socializing event than a forum for acknowledging God. I miss the art of worship. I miss the beating of drums, the shaking of tambourines and the stringing of guitars. I miss seeing the choir as they worship the Lord in song. This art of worship often helped me engage and feel the presence of God. I would leave church not only feeling happy, but feeling blessed.

Some of practices carried out amongst my husband's religious men

My husband often tells me his religious leaders have called him to help pacify an issue between members from his community. This occurs when someone has made unkind or accusatory remarks about an individual or individuals. Instead of the community judging the individual or individuals, they call a meeting, in which all the involved parties have their say until the issue is rectified. This was what I had expected from the church. My husband explained to me that all problems in the community were handled in this manner. According to Maqsood (2008), Muslims believe that only God has the right to pass judgment on any one, as it's only God that can judge fairly. However, I am not sure if this is practiced amongst Muslims the world over. This has been my experience from the people that I have been exposed to from both the Christian and Islamic faith.

On the other hand, although most Christian parents wouldn't be happy if their child converted to Islam, it's unlikely that they would ostracize them. My mother loves me no less than she did at the time of my birth. She's no less supportive of me and continues to believe in me as a person, as well as to encourage me to strive for the best in life. I am sure that during her moments of prayer, she has put me before God and asked for His divine intervention in helping me to make the right choice religiously. The same cannot be said about someone from the Islamic faith who changes his religion. This behavior is unacceptable to Muslims, and most who convert find that they are isolated from their families due to the widely held belief that leaving the Muslim faith is immoral (Maqsood, 2008).

I don't have typical attire for Islamic women in my wardrobe, as I have a varied dress sense and like to experiment with different types of clothing. I do admire the manner in which women are covered when attending the mosque, as this shows reverence to God. In the Caribbean, a woman wouldn't enter a church with her head uncovered or any parts of her body on display. Now, it seems that women enter the house of God in the same attire they'd wear to a nightclub. People don't seem to fear God anymore in the Christian world, whilst respect and worship for God continues to be at the center of Islamic belief.

The differences in burial

I have tried my best to be a decent human being, and I have worked hard to achieve the things I have. When my time on earth is ended, I would love to be given a burial that will please the loved ones I have left behind. I would also like to look on from the spirit world and say, 'I am pleased with the effort that my loved ones made in ensuring that my final resting place was given a flare of the style that I was so accustomed to having whilst on earth.' I would love for my body to be buried in an elegant and well-polished coffin. I'd love to have an exquisite wreath with statements of love written on it. If I should pass on before my mom and my daughter, I would love for them to accompany my body to the burial ground, as I believe this will give closure to the loved ones left behind.

However, in the Islamic world, females aren't allowed to attend the burial site. They pay their last respects to their loved ones before they leave for burial. This is of great concern to me, as I know that my mother would be mortified if she wasn't able to pay her last respect to me at my burial site, if I should pass away before her. She wouldn't be able to forgive me and I don't think that she would be able to move on, knowing that the daughter she raised helped to alienate and rob her from paying her last respect. In equal measures, it would be heart wrenching for me, if my daughter and I weren't able to stand at my husband's, (her dad) burial site, giving each other support and paying our last respect. It doesn't have the same meaning to me, saying good bye to a loved one who has passed away at the home or funeral home. It doesn't seem final somehow.

My Conversion to Islam

On the day of my conversion, I had mixed emotions. I was happy because I was taking a step closer to marrying the man I so loved. However, I was also taking on a new religion that was different from the faith that I was raised with. I still felt anger towards the church for defaming my mother. If they hadn't inflicted so much pain, if they had been 'Christ-like,' if the pastor or the deacons would have had the spiritual eyes to see that what was being said were all lies, or if they would have had sufficient knowledge about their roles and acted their parts, then my mother would have been vindicated. And maybe, I wouldn't feel the need to find strength from another religion.

My conversion was conducted at a mosque. I didn't understand most of what was said, as the service was conducted in Arabic. However, I knew that I went in a Christian and came out a Muslim. On my journey home, I couldn't get thoughts of my mother out of my head. Although she was supportive of my decision, I knew she was doing it because she wanted me to be happy. I couldn't help but think of how painful it must have been for her to see the child that she had raised and the beliefs that she had raised her with suddenly become altered. I felt guilty and confused, as no one outside the Islamic faith thought I had made the right decision. Non-Muslims said things like, 'You won't be able to cope,' 'You're not used to that lifestyle,' and, 'You'll be imprisoned; he'll stop you from seeing your mom.' I was concerned about marrying someone who might interfere with my relationship with my mother, but I wasn't marrying a stranger. I was marrying my best friend, and I knew him well. He wasn't anything like what others' assumed.

Arriving home, I felt what I could only describe as the presence of God. I had felt this before. It was a warm sensation running through my body, which I had experienced during an altar call back home in Jamaica. I had no doubt about what had just happened; however, I was confused about why I had felt the presence of God at home and not at the mosque. Still, I knew there and then that I had not done anything wrong. Despite all the negative comments and discouragement I'd received, my confirmation was here. My conversion to Islam was not an abomination. I felt the presence of God, which for me was an acknowledgement from God that I had chosen the right path.

I immediately told my mother about my experience. She thought this phenomenal experience had occurred because she had been praying for me so that the presence of the Lord was in the house when I returned from the mosque. This could have been another explanation, but I've held on to my initial belief to this very day. I spoke to Ibrahim about my experience, and he told me that he had encountered the same sensation when he visited Mecca. 'One has to be holy in order to have such an experience,' he explained. 'The fact that you felt this on the day of your conversion means that God is pleased with your doings.' I was so excited. As at last, I could accept that God hadn't turned away from me, nor was I living a life that was unacceptable to him. However, I feared mentioning the presence of God on me on the day of my conversion to anyone else for fear of reprisal, so I kept quiet for many years.

Chapter 5

My Wedding Day

We decided that we would have our wedding ceremony in August 2005 and have our marriage registered at a registrar's office with close family and friends at a later date. On the day of the August ceremony, I arrived at the hall in a limousine. I wore a traditional ivory dress made by my mom with a flowing veil and tiara. I didn't wear a hejab, as some people assumed I would. For my reception, I wore an African two-piece outfit. My husband wore a three-piece African outfit for the ceremony and a two-piece African gown for the reception. He looked immaculate in both outfits. Two imams and several sheiks conducted the ceremony.

The attendance was a mixture of Afro-Caribbean Christians and African Muslims. Not all the invitees from my culture attended the wedding, as they had made it clear that they did not approve of my marriage. During the ceremony, my husband had to arrive before me, as is done in a Christian marriage. I had to have a father figure to give me away, but he had to be a Muslim. This made it impossible for me to choose anyone from my family. Instead, I gave my consent to have a figure selected for me. He was an Afro-Caribbean from Antigua who had converted to Islam along with his wife and kids. Instead of walking me down the aisle, my 'give-away dad' was already seated in the room with my husband and the other guests. I walked down the aisle to absolute silence, as opposed to a hymn, as practiced in Christianity.

I approached a room that had a congregation of both men and women, with no segregation according to sex. I sat beside my mother as the ceremony began. I could see my husband across the room, seated at a different table. I wasn't allowed to join him until we were considered husband and wife. When the imams spoke, an English speaker translated their Arabic for us. I have never received so much prayer in my life; I felt eternally blessed.

My mother was asked to give a speech. She spoke about my upbringing and my faith. She emphasized that everyone in the room, 'whether Christian or Muslim, should remember both Ibrahim and Linnette in their prayers.' I was so proud. My mom had spoken respectfully about a religion that was so scorned upon from those in her own world. And even though a handful of them attended the wedding, that did not keep her from demonstrating her loyalty and love for me. When we exchanged rings, a prayer from one of the imams replaced the traditional, 'with this ring, I thee wed,' speech.

Although the ceremony was different in parts to what I was accustomed to, I felt that it was a success. My husband and I left the room, followed by the other guests. We got in the limousine and went to take pictures. We later returned to the reception in our African outfits. This again was a success; however, the cutting of the cake wasn't incorporated within the reception ceremony. My husband explained to me that to partake of cakes at an Islamic wedding was prohibited. It was never explained to me, as to why this was prohibited and I didn't question this.

The event was over, and we left to live as husband and wife even though I couldn't legally announce myself as his wife. We were married in the eyes of the Islamic world, but we still had further wedding plans to arrange. On the day of the civil ceremony, which was arrange for the month of January, I invited only my mother, and my husband invited a few of his family members. The ceremony was conducted in a traditional manner. In January of 2006, I legally became Mrs. Sow.

My Trip to Guinea

My husband and I visited Guinea, where the rest of his family resides. I had never seen poverty on such a wide scale, but nor have I ever experienced so much love from any other country. Even though the people of Guinea didn't have a lot of material wealth, they were adamant that you should not leave a visit without accepting a gift. I was given a live chicken on one occasion and some mangoes on another. However, amongst this wealth of generosity, I couldn't help but notice that this was a culture that relished having multiple wives. Four out of five of the homes we visited had more than one wife in residence, with vast amounts of kids. These kids would refer to their father's wives who were not their mothers, as 'aunties.' Each woman would take it in turn to greet me. 'Are they sisters?' I asked my husband.

'No, they're mates,' he responded. I couldn't help but notice that the body language of most of these women expressed the conflict and unhappiness in their household. Most of these women were living under the same roof and sharing the same man as their husband, but they were clearly archenemies. One home in particular struck me, as both women were competing to serve my husband and me hot drinks; we ended up having two cups of tea each.

I questioned my husband about this lifestyle. I was aware that within the Islamic faith it was acceptable for a man to have more than one wife. But how difficult this must have been for the wives! My husband explained that having multiple wives was acceptable if a man could emotionally and financially meet the needs of them equally. But it was clear to see that these men could hardly meet and maintain their own needs, let alone two wives and several kids.

This cycle of poverty would only be passed on to the next generation. Most of the women didn't work, and therefore relied on their husbands for financial well-being—even if they were so impoverished that they couldn't afford a meal every night. I felt sorry for these women and children, as I came to realized that their predicament wasn't self-inflicted; nor did they have a choice about their future, as the men they married and the life they lived were all predetermined for them by their elders of whom are normally predominantly male. In most cases, this would be determined by their fathers. However, if their fathers were deceased, then an uncle/uncles would make this decision for them. Some of these girls were getting married as young as thirteen.

The men would not help around the house, but there was no need for that, as they had two wives and several children to carry out tasks for them. The men were the breadwinners, even if they weren't taking home enough bread to feed the household. The kids seemed happy and oblivious to both their poverty and their mothers' unhappiness. They would congregate in the yard every evening after school and play with their half sisters and brothers without resentment or malice.

Although I was taken aback by the culture and lifestyle of the Guinea people, I enjoyed my stay there. There wasn't anyone to fabricate stories about me, nor was there anyone to be prejudiced about the Christian friends I'd chosen to keep. For the first time in many years, I felt at peace. I remembered what happiness was and cherished every moment of it.

My Experience of Muslim Family in England

Back in England, where many of my husband's countrymen lived, I realized that they didn't share the same views about multiple marriages as the Muslims in Guinea. Was this because they weren't legally allowed to have more than one wife in Britain? Or was it simply that people were exposed to a different way of life in England? Despite these differences, I also observed similarities between British and Guinean Muslims. The men in England were predominantly the breadwinners, whilst the women were happy to stay at home, rear the children, and take care of their husbands.

I had come from a background where not only was my mother the sole breadwinner for the home, but she also played the role of being both my mother and father, as my father was hardly ever in my life. She was self-sufficient and very independent. She ran our home without help or hand-outs from anyone. She did a fantastic job of bringing me up on her own. I was always well groomed before going to school, church and other functions. And I never had to do without. I was used to a woman being the head of the home and making all the decisions. Anything different from this wasn't normal to me.

The Muslim women I had close encounters with seemed unable to make decisions without their husbands' consent. Something as simple as buying a dress, called for a husband's approval before a woman did it. Once, I was with my husband when I saw some African dresses on sale. When I showed interest in one, another woman said, 'Ask your husband first.' I found this behavior quite bizarre, but I concealed my disbelief.

To many of these women, their husbands are their greatest achievements, and the more children they have, the more successful they are considered to be. Whilst most of these women were seemingly happy, I couldn't help but notice that a small minority were terrible unhappy. They demonstrated this by their obnoxious behavior towards me that derived from jealousy. One woman made as many impertinent comments as she possible could towards me. All but one of these comments didn't bother me, as I realized that her remarks stemmed from the fact that I was everything she was not. After all, I was a university graduate with a BSc (hons) degree, I owned a car and I was financially able to run my home equally with my husband.

On one of her visits to my home, this particular woman asked to see my wedding album. As she went through it, she saw photos of me in my wedding dress. She asked, 'Did your mom make your wedding dress?'

'Yes!' I replied as she continued to plough through my wedding album.

She came across a picture of my mother wearing a two-piece, tailor-made outfit. 'Are you going to say that she made this, as well?' she asked, implying that I was lying. I realized the connotation behind the comment, but I succeeded in suppressing my emotions. I have always found it difficult to be in her presence, but after this comment, I realized that she was also bitter and rude. I therefore did my best to avoid her, as I did not wish to engage in battle.

Chapter 6

My Fear for my Daughter

My husband and I have a beautiful baby girl. My hope for her is that she will be able to make informed choices when she reaches adulthood. This includes choices about religion. She was born in a multicultural society and will very likely be raised within that society. She will be exposed to and will have interaction with kids from different religions and cultures. And with religion now being apart of the school curriculum, my daughter will be far more educated than her dad and me about it.

She's also from two different cultures, her mom being a Jamaican Christian and her dad being an African Muslim. I will ensure that she grows up with an awareness of both cultures. And whatever religion she chooses to practice, I will give her my support. However, I will teach her the advantages and disadvantages of both worlds. I will be as open and honest as I possibly can be. I will inform her that as a Christian, she may find herself defamed. If she decides to become a Muslim, she may find that the non-Muslim world will distance themselves from her out of prejudice.

My other concern for my daughter is that she may never be able to own either of her parents' religions or cultures, or that she might struggle for acceptance from both worlds. They may even refuse to accept that she shares any part in either world.

I fear that she might become another Ruksana, ostracized by non-Muslims because of her religion. Even after we have come far enough as a society that individuals of many different colors can sit at the same table and enjoy a meal, we still hate and fear what we don't know or understand.

My Marriage

I have been blessed in my marriage. I can proudly say that I have the most supportive, loving, caring and understanding husband. He's not only my companion, but my best friend. I can depend on his support in everything I do. Shortly after giving birth to my daughter, I decided to study MSc in nursing. However, this course was being run thirty-five miles from home. My baby was only three months old and purely breast-fed. My husband took annual leave for the days that I had class and commuted with me and our baby. He would take her to my mom, who lived in the same county that I was undertaking my master's programme, until it was time for her to feed. He would then drive her to the university where I was studying so she could feed before he returned to my mom with her.

He's been my rock and supporter in everything I have done. Even if it means that he has to put aside his dreams, he'll do just that if it makes me happy. Whenever I don't have the confidence to take on a particular task, he convinces me that I can. He makes the time to celebrate my mom's birthday and Mother's Day. Although he doesn't celebrate Christmas, he visits my mother with me on Christmas Day.

Most of all, I adore the manner in which he loves our daughter. He's totally a hands-on father. He never tries to avoid changing her nappies or giving her a bath. He's up with her in the mornings whether it's 02.00 a.m. or 06.30 a.m., whether she's feeling unwell or thinking it's time to play. Once at the hair salon, I mentioned my husband's technique for changing our daughter's diapers. In disbelief, the women in the salon asked whether my husband really changed our daughter's diapers. 'Why wouldn't he? She's his daughter,' I said.

'I didn't think he would. Muslim men aren't domesticated, and they think it's beneath them to help around the house,' replied one woman. I wondered how she could think a population of thousands of men could all be the same.

I found myself often on the defensive during the early years of my marriage. People spoke about it as though I wasn't in their presence. Most of these people have never met my husband, but because he's Muslim, they think they have the right to be completely impertinent to my family.

The irony is that some of these women passing judgment were in volatile and abusive relationships, receiving regular visits from the police due to domestic abuse, or they were unmarried and had multiple kids with multiple partners. Here I am, married to a decent, educated human being who has a degree in psychology and a diploma in mental health nursing. He's a man who's worked as hard as he can to ensure that his family is well looked after. And because he's a believer of the Islamic faith, people talk about him in a manner that portrays him as uncaring, controlling and primitive. If only these people could spend a day in my house and see the type of person he really is!

The Internal Conflict

A part of me wishes I could incorporate certain aspects of my Christian upbringing with my newfound religion. There are parts of Christianity I miss and other parts that, to this day, I refuse to not be a part of. There will always be a conflict; I know the two religions can never be one because Muslims don't share the fundamental teaching of Christianity that God is the Father, the Son and the Holy Spirit (1 John 5:1–12).

My mom and I attended a Pastor Benny Hinn Gospel Crusade in France in the 1990s. Pastor Benny Hinn is known as one of the most powerful men of God. Through the Holy Spirit, he has healed people with illnesses that doctors have given a prognosis of death. Mom and I attended this crusade because Mom was unwell physically, and we hoped by attending, it would bring a miracle to heal Mom. During the crusade, Pastor Benny Hinn made an altar call. Mom and I both obeyed; this was the reason we had come. Pastor Benny Hinn later announced that he was going to ask the Holy Spirit to present Himself as a ball of fire and pass over the palms of the congregators' hands. All we had to do was to stretch our hands out, he emphasized.

Even before I finished stretching out my hands, I felt a warm sensation in the palm of my left hand. My legs gave way beneath me, and I began to fall. If a complete stranger hadn't broken my fall, I would have ended up on the floor. I began to shake, whilst tears poured from my eyes. I felt as though an electric current was passing through my body! This encounter lasted about five minutes. This was an extraordinary experience—the Spirit of God manifesting Himself through me. This experience left me feeling weak and tired. I told my mom that I wasn't sure why the Spirit of God was upon me, as I wasn't sick; however, I didn't think my life would ever be the same after this encounter.

This is an experience I will never forget. I felt blessed, honored and privileged! Unbelievers, psychiatrists and even my colleagues may question my mental health. But if this is the experience one has in a psychotic phase, then I wouldn't mind being psychotic for the rest of my life. Sadly, I have never had this experience again. But after such an experience, how could I not believe in God the Holy Spirit?

However, I adore the unfading respect the Islamic faith has for God. This is demonstrated in the way they pray and in their dress when visiting a mosque. Respect for God amongst Christians has become diluted amongst people of my generation. If you were given the opportunity to meet God in person, would you turn up with your cleavage and underwear on display? Of course you wouldn't. You'd ensure that you were well groomed and in your best attire. So why don't we all come to God's 'house' (church) in this manner?

As for me, I have come to the conclusion that I don't need to attend a specific religious building to have a faith. I don't need to be part of a congregation to believe in God. Most importantly, I am no less important in God's eyes for not being a member of a church or a mosque.

My Hope for the Future

I hope that one day the world we live in will be far more accepting of differences. We will realize that whether we say 'God' or 'Allah,' we are all the same in the Creator's eyes. On Judgment Day, we will be judged according to the life we have lived on earth: the good deeds we have done for our neighbors and the help we have given our brothers.

God is love, and if He can love us all equally, wherever we are from, whatever our background, credentials or society, why can't we do the same unto one another? If we aim to be like Him, then first we must accept one another.

References

The Holy Bible New International Version; the Books of the Old Testament, International Bible Society, 2001.

Collins Gem, *English Dictionary* (1994) Harpers Collins Publishers.

Dr. Al Hilali Muhammad Taqi-ud-Din., Dr. Khan Muhammad Muhsin.(1984) *Translation of the meanings of The Noble Qur'an In the English Language*, King Fahd Complex for the printing of the Holy Qur'an, Madinah, K.S.A

http://www.carm.org/christianity/baptism/ (03/04/2009) Should-we baptize-name-father-son-and-holy-spirit

http://www.allaboutreligion.org (03/04/2009) Definition-of-religion-fac.htm.

http://www.carm.org/christianity/answers-seeking/what-christianity (03/04/2009)

Ibrahim I. A. (1997) *A Brief Illustrated Guide to understanding Islam*). 2nd Ed, Houston, Texas, USA.

The Qur'an, Basic Teachings, (1984) The Islamic foundation, Revised Edition, Ashford Colour Press LTd. Gasport, Hants.

(Maqsood W. R. (2008). *Need to know? Islam, Understand the religion behind the* headlines. Harper Collins, Publisher.

48

www.ingramcontent.com/pod-product-compliance
Lightning Source LLC
Chambersburg PA
CBHW022122090426
42743CB00008B/964